Rabbits

Rabbits are cute, cuddly, gentle, friendly, and easy to take care of.

DID YOU KNOW?

All rabbits originated from European rabbits in the Middle Ages, when they were domesticated. A pet rabbit can live up to 10 years and its teeth never stop growing. A young rabbit is called a *kit*, while a young hare is called a *leveret*. A male is a *buck* and a female is a *doe*.

Pug

A Pug is cute and affectionate, but very opinionated!

Pugs originated in Asia around 400 B.C. They are one of the oldest dog breeds. In the 16th century, Pugs were the pets of European royalty. Even Napoleon's wife, Josephine, had a Pug. They weigh up to 18 lbs. (8 kg) and are about 11 in. (28 cm) in length.

American shorthair

In 948 A.D., it was against the law to kill a cat. The penalty was as much grain as the cat was long.

DID YOU KNOW?

American Shorthairs were derived from European wildcats and arrived in North America in the 1600s. American Shorthairs are strong, muscled, and great mousers! They can weigh more than 10 lbs. (4.5 kg).

Dalmatian and Labrador Retriever

The Dalmatian and the Labrador Retriever are alert, hard-working, yet playful dogs.

DID YOU KNOW?

Dalmatians originated in India. They are active, fast, and intelligent. This dog loves to be around horses and was once a follower and guardian of horse-drawn vehicles. They can grow to be 23 in. (58 cm) high at the shoulder.

The Labrador Retriever is originally from Newfoundland, where it helped fishermen pull in nets. This popular dog has fur that comes in yellow, brown, and black. Labradors can weigh up to 75 lbs. (34 kg).

Poodle

The Poodle is exceptionally smart and active.

Poodles originated in Germany as a water dog. The Poodle haircut became popular because the tufts of hair protect vital organs and joints from the cold water. A Poodle comes in three sizes: toy, miniature, and medium. Toy Poodles often performed in the circus.

Mixed-Breed Cats

The world's largest mixed-breed cat is from Australia. The cat, named Himmy, weighs 47 lbs. (21 kg) and is 41 in. (104 cm) in length from the top of its head to the tip of its tail.

DID YOU KNOW?

A mixed-breed cat is a feline whose parents are two different breeds. Like all cats, a mixed-breed kitten is born blind and helpless. Mixed-breed cats are instinctively clean and will use the litter box as young as three weeks old.

PIG

Pigs wallow in the mud to keep cool and protect themselves from sunburn, but they really are clean animals!

DID YOU KNOW?

Pigs were domesticated in Asia from wild boars as early as 13,000 B.C. Today, they are even kept as pets. They are distantly related to the hippopotamus. A female pig is called a *sow*, and a male is called a *boar*. A baby pig is called a *piglet*. The largest pig weighed 2,552 lbs. (1,158 kg).

Schnauzer

The Schnauzer was named after its most noticeable feature, the nose, which in German is "schnauze."

Schnauzers originated in Germany in the 1400s. This dog is sturdy and athletic, but sociable and affectionate, too. It is naturally protective. There are three breeds of Schnauzer—the Miniature, the Standard, and the Giant.

Cow

A dairy cow can eat almost 100 lbs. (45 kg) of food and drink up to 50 gal. (189 L) of water each day!

DID YOU KNOW?

In 1611, the first cow arrived in America at the Jamestown Colony. They have been domesticated for thousands of years. A cow is a ruminant animal with four digestive compartments to its stomach. It chews *cud* (partially digested food) for up to eight hours each day.

Kittens

Kittens cannot hear for two weeks after they are born.

A group of kittens is called a *kindle*. Cats normally have up to five kittens in a litter, but the largest litter was 19 kittens. Only mother cats can safely pick up their own kittens by the scruff of the neck.

Ferret

The word *ferret* comes from the Latin word "Furonem," which means thief.

DID YOU KNOW?

Ferrets have been domesticated for more than 2,500 years. There are stories of Genghis Khan using ferrets in 1221. A ferret is a relative of the weasel and the European polecat. Ferrets are born blind, deaf, and without hair. As adults, they can weigh up to 6 lbs. (2.7 kg).

chicks

Chicks recognize their mother by the noises she makes.

Chickens originated in Southeast Asia from a wild species of jungle fowl. There are more than 100 breeds of chickens today. National Geographic scientists believe the egg came first, because reptiles were laying eggs way before a chicken appeared.

French Bulldogs

These dogs snore because of their flat face.

DID YOU KNOW?

In the 1800s, French Bulldogs first appeared in France. They earned the nickname "frog dogs" because of the way they lie with their legs spread out behind them. These dogs are cute and cuddly, but a little stubborn. French Bulldogs were fancied by royalty throughout history, and one unfortunate dog was a passenger on the *Titanic*.

Cat

A cat's ear has 30 muscles. These muscles rotate so the cat can hear in all directions without moving its head.

DID YOU KNOW?

Cats' whiskers act like feelers. They help the cat judge how big a space is so kitty can tell whether or not it can fit into the space. A cat's sharp claws are its weapon and retract (pull back) when the cat isn't using them. This is also very effective in allowing the cat to creep silently. If they didn't retract, their claws would make noise like a dog's.

Kitten, DUCK and Rabbit

Kittens, ducks, and rabbits are kept as pets for companionship.

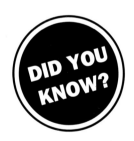

Humans have enjoyed the love and affection from pets like kittens, ducks, and rabbits for as long as anyone can remember.

Piglets

A mother pig can have a litter of 8 to 12 piglets, and she can have two litters each year.

Some piglets have straight tails, while others have curly tails. A piglet weighs about 3 lbs. (1.5 kg) at birth. The smallest piglet of a litter is called a *runt*. Piglets will run in zig-zag lines in order to get away from predators.

Chicks

It takes 21 days for a chicken egg to hatch.

DID YOU KNOW?

Chicks need to have the air temperature at 95°F (35°C) at all times during their first week of life. They peep loudly when they are too cold. Chicks sleep most of the time, just like a human baby.

SQUIRREL

There are more than 365 species of squirrels around the world.

DID YOU KNOW?

Squirrels have been around for a long time. Fossilized squirrel bones date back about 37 million years. Modern squirrels belong to the rodent family. Squirrel babies are usually born in the spring each year. A baby squirrel weighs about 1 oz. (28 g) at birth.

French Bulldog

French Bulldogs are not good swimmers because they are top-heavy.

In the 19th century, lace makers in England bred a smaller bulldog as a companion. When the lace makers moved to France, they brought the dogs with them. "Frenchies," as they are commonly called, are affectionate and active, and they love snuggling in your lap.

Kitten and Duck

Many cat breeds enjoy the water as much as a duck, including the Turkish Van, Maine Coon, and Egyptian Mau.

DID YOU KNOW?

Throughout the world, there are stories of mother cats adopting ducklings. One story tells of a mother duck that was out walking her seven ducklings when a cat approached. The mother duck quickly ushered her ducklings into the water, only to leave one stranded with the cat. The cat gently lifted the tiny bird in her mouth and carried it home. The cat raised the duckling as lovingly as she would her own kittens.

Rabbit

Angora wool doesn't come from sheep. It is actually from the Angora rabbit.

The Angora rabbit is one of the oldest breeds of domestic rabbits. They were popular pets with French royalty in the 1700s. Angoras are bred for their long, soft hair. They look like a fur ball.

Shih Tzu

The Shih Tzu is a friendly, trusting lap dog that at one time lived with Chinese royalty.

The word *Shih Tzu* means "lion," but this dog is cute, sweet, and playful. It is one of the most popular dogs in the U.S. Shih Tzus are true house pets. They don't require a lot of exercise and love to curl up in your lap.

CatS and DOgS

Cats and dogs have been pets for thousands of years. So, what is the difference between cats and dogs?

DID YOU KNOW?

Cats are independent and extremely territorial, while a pack (a group of dogs) is more important to a dog. Cats learn by smelling and exploring the territory, but dogs learn by observing and being part of a pack. Cats are fast and agile, and they run away when they get scared. A dog will turn and fight when frightened.